Dear Sis Let's Walk This Out Together

From My Heart to Yours:
A 31-Day Devotional of Faith, Hope, and Healing

Dr. Tache' Vereen

Dear Sis: Let's Walk This Out Together — From My Heart to Yours: A 31-Day Devotional of Faith, Hope, and Healing

Book Cover & Layout Design: Abu Bakar Javed

Published by DOC with TV LLC
www.docwithtv.com

ISBN: 979-8-9993418-0-8

Acknowledgments

First off, I want to give glory to God—my Everything! Without Him, I would be nothing. I thank Him for placing the thought of writing this devotional on my heart and for walking with me every step of the way.

To my husband and my children—your existence inspires me daily to become a better version of myself. Thank you for your love, patience, and constant encouragement.

To my friends and my sister circle—thank you for always being there when I needed you the most. Your words of encouragement, your prayers, and the space you give me to simply be me mean more than I can express.

To my spiritual leaders and mentors—thank you for pouring into me and covering me throughout my journey with the Lord. Your wisdom and support helped shapes this devotional.

To every woman—my spiritual sister—who will read this devotional, thank you. You were on my heart with every word and every prayer. I pray this book meets you in your season and reminds you that you're never alone.

And lastly, to anyone who spoke a word of encouragement, prayed a silent prayer, or believed in me—thank you from the bottom of my heart.

Table of Contents

Introduction

Dear Sis,

I'm so glad you're here. I want you to know this devotional was written with you in mind—with love, prayer, and the kind of understanding that comes from walking through some things.

I've been in seasons where I just needed someone to walk with me. Someone to talk to. Someone who gets it. Life as a parent, a wife, a woman trying to stay rooted in God while juggling it all... I understand the weight. I also understand the beauty of having someone say, *"I'm with you."*

That's what "Dear Sis" is all about. It's more than just a title—it's a heartfelt invitation. A love letter from one sister to another. A space where we can be real about our faith, our struggles, our victories, and everything in between. I may not know you by name, but we're connected—through grace, through hope, and through our shared journey with God.

This 31-day devotional is here to encourage you, strengthen your faith, and remind you that you're not walking alone. If you need to pause and sit with a particular day—do that. If a prayer or reflection prompts you to cry, rejoice, or pray a little deeper—lean into it. Let the Holy Spirit guide your pace. This is your sacred space with God.

And as we walk this out together, let these words remind you: you are loved, you are seen, and you are never alone.

With love,
Your sister in Christ
Dr. Tache' Vereen

Isaiah 30:21 (AMP)
"Your ears will hear a word behind you, saying, 'This is the way, walk in it,' whenever you turn to the right or to the left."

How to Use This 31- Day Devotional

This devotional is meant to be read one day at a time, but Sis, I want you to move at your own pace. Some days, God may have you pause and sit a little longer. Other days, you may feel ready to move forward. That's okay—follow His lead.

Here's how I recommend using this devotional each day:

- **Start with prayer.** Invite the Holy Spirit into your time and space.

- **Read the Scripture.** Let the Word wash over you—don't rush it.

- **Read the "Dear Sis" entry.** Picture me sitting with you, just talking and sharing heart to heart.

- **Pray the prayer.** Use it as a starting point, then talk to God in your own words too.

- **Reflect and worship.** Sit with the prompt. Journal, pray, or just be still—whatever you need. Look up and listen to the song suggestion. Let the music minister to your soul. Sometimes God speaks the loudest through a melody.

If you don't feel led to move to the next day—don't. Maybe God is doing something deep. Stay there. Let Him finish what He started. This isn't a checklist—it's a journey with Jesus.

Let this devotional be your quiet place, your safe space, your soul refresh. *And remember*—I'm walking with you, Sis.

A Prayer of Blessing

Father,

I lift up my sister to You as she steps into this journey of faith. Heal her in the places only You can reach. Strengthen her when life feels heavy and overwhelming. Lead her when the path is unclear, and guide her when decisions must be made.

As she reads each daily entry and meets with You, fill her with more of Your Spirit. Cover her mind, her heart, and her home with Your peace and protection. I speak blessings over her life, her purpose, and her walk with You.

Keep her, Lord. In Jesus' name, amen.

> **Numbers 6:24–26 (NKJV)**
> *"The Lord bless you and keep you; The Lord make His face shine upon you,*
> *And be gracious to you; The Lord lift up His countenance upon you,*
> *And give you peace."*

Day 1:   Living in His Peace

Scripture:

"Then you will experience God's peace, which exceeds anything we can understand. His peace will guard your hearts and minds as you live in Christ Jesus."
— Philippians 4:7 NLT

Dear Sis,

Life is full of highs and lows—seasons of joy and moments of hardship. Whether we welcome them or not, challenges will come. But in the midst of it all, God offers us something the world simply cannot: His peace.

We may not always understand the *what,* the *why,* or the *how* behind our circumstances. Life doesn't always make sense—but God does. *But God!* In every situation, He extends a supernatural peace that calms the storms and quiets our hearts.

But here's the key: His peace comes when we live in Him. Stay connected. Make Him not just your Savior, but your source, your anchor, your everything. It's in the abiding—remaining in His presence—that peace flows like a river and steadies your soul.

He's waiting—with open arms and perfect peace.

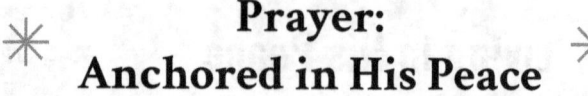

Prayer:
Anchored in His Peace

Father God,

Your Word promises that Your peace will guard my heart and my mind as I live in You—and today, I choose to receive that peace. Life may bring storms, but I choose to face them wrapped in Your perfect presence.

When the weight of life presses in, help me to lift my eyes to You. Keep me rooted in Your Word and anchored in Your Spirit. I declare that I will stay connected, remain faithful, and trust You—even when the path is unclear.

I choose to live in You, Lord. I choose to stay—especially when it's hard—because I know You hold the answers, and You hold me.

Thank You for being my peace, my guide, my God.
In Jesus' name, amen.

Reflect and Worship

♫ **Song Suggestion:**
He Kept Me
— Lamont Sanders

Sis, as you reflect on today's devotional, take a moment to worship with this song. Let the lyrics remind you that God's keeping power is real and ever-present. Look it up on your favorite music platform and let it minister to your heart today.

Reflection Prompt:

Where in your life do you need God's peace the most today? What can you do to stay connected to Him in that area?

_____

_____

_____

_____

_____

_____

_____

_____

_____

_____

_____

_____

_____

_____

_____

_____

_____

_____

Day 2: Speak Life, Walk in Authority

Scripture:

"The tongue can bring death or life; those who love to talk will reap the consequences."
— *Proverbs 18:21 NLT*

Dear Sis,

As women of God, we must be mindful not to be led by our emotions, but by the Spirit of God within us. Yes, emotions are real—but they are not always right. In those heated moments of fear, frustration, or anxiety, take a step back. Pause. Breathe. Pray. Let the Holy Spirit settle your heart before you release your words.

Why? Because your words carry weight.

The Bible reminds us that life and death are in the power of the tongue. What you speak has the ability to build up or break down. You're not just talking—you're creating atmosphere. So be intentional. Speak hope. Speak truth. Speak God's Word.

You have been given divine authority. Walk in it.

You are not at the mercy of your emotions—you are led by the Spirit. And when you align your voice with Heaven, strongholds break, peace reigns, and things begin to shift.

Use your words wisely, Sis. Speak life over yourself, your family, your situation, and your home. The power is already in you.

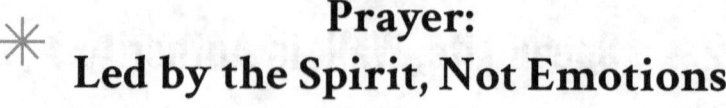

Prayer:
Led by the Spirit, Not Emotions

Father God,

Lord, when I feel overwhelmed, anxious, or frustrated, help me to pause and turn to You. Don't let me speak out of my emotions—teach me to speak from a place of peace and spiritual authority.

Your Word says that life and death are in the power of the tongue. So I ask You, Father, train my mouth to speak life. Let my words reflect faith and not fear. Let them build and not destroy. I want to align with Heaven's language and not let my feelings override Your plans.

I surrender my voice, my emotions, and my heart to You. Lead me by Your Spirit, and help me walk daily in the authority You've given me. In Jesus' name, amen.

Reflect and Worship

🎵 **Song Suggestion:**
Just Saying What He Said (feat. Chaquanna Iman)
— Travis Greene & Forward City

Let this song be your declaration today, Sis. God's promises are true, and when you repeat what He says, your faith grows stronger. Find this worship moment on your go-to music app and let it lift your spirit.

Reflection Prompt:

What have you been speaking over your life lately? Is it life-giving or draining? How can you begin to shift your words to align with God's truth?

_____

_____

_____

_____

_____

_____

_____

_____

_____

_____

_____

_____

_____

_____

_____

_____

_____

_____

_____

Day 3:   Sis, Don't Give Up

Scripture:
*"But as for you, be strong and courageous,
for your work will be rewarded."*
— 2 Chronicles 15:7 NLT

Dear Sis,

Don't stop now—you're closer than you think.

God sees you. He sees every tear you've cried, every prayer you've whispered, every time you've chosen to believe when it would've been easier to quit. He knows what you're facing, and He hasn't forgotten about you.

This is not the time to walk away. This is the time to lean in.

Your breakthrough may be just around the corner. Every seed you've sown in faith, every act of obedience, every moment you stayed when you could've given up—it matters. God is working, even when you can't see it.

Sis, don't give up.

You've come too far to turn back now. There's more ahead of you than behind you. Yes, it's hard. Yes, the weight feels heavy. But you're not alone. I'm praying for you—and more importantly, God is with you.

Keep pushing. Keep believing. Keep standing on His promises.
Because God is faithful, and He always keeps His Word.

Prayer:
Strength to Keep Going

Father God,

Thank You for being the God who sees me—every struggle, every battle, every silent cry.

Lord, Your Word reminds me to be strong and courageous, for my work will be rewarded. Strengthen my heart today. Help me to keep going, even when I feel like giving up. Let me hold on to the truth that You are working on my behalf—even in the unseen.

When the road gets tough, be my strength. When I'm tired, renew my spirit. Remind me that my labor is not in vain and that Your promises are yes and amen.

I choose to believe. I choose to push. I choose to stand.
In Jesus' name, amen.

Reflect and Worship

🎵 **Song Suggestion:**
Turning Around For Me
— VaShawn Mitchell

Let this song remind you that God is always ready to turn things around in your life. Whenever you feel stuck or discouraged, find this worship moment on your favorite music app and let it encourage your heart.

Reflection Prompt:

What situation in your life needs God's turnaround today? How can you trust Him more in that area?

Day 4: Equipped Through the Word

Scripture: 2 Timothy 3:16–17 (NLT)

*"All Scripture is inspired by God and is useful to teach us what is true
and to make us realize what is wrong in our lives. It corrects us
when we are wrong and teaches us to do what is right.
God uses it to prepare and to equip his people to do every good work."*

Dear Sis,

There is power in the Word of God. Every verse, every line, every page carries purpose and power. Scripture is not just ink on paper—it is God's truth, and heart extended toward you. The Bible teaches us what is true and helps us recognize what needs to be refined within us. It is God's tool to shape, equip, and grow you into the woman He created you to be.

Start small if you must—one verse a day, one quiet moment with Him. What matters is the consistency of your pursuit. As you read, invite the Holy Spirit to reveal, correct, comfort, and strengthen you. Don't aim for perfection, Sis—aim for connection. Let the Word work in your heart and mind, guiding your decisions and transforming your life.

You are a work in progress, and that's okay. God is preparing you for every good work He's called you to. Stay rooted in His Word, and you will begin to see the fruit of your obedience.

Prayer:
Make Me Better, Lord

Father God, thank You for the gift of Your Word—it is alive, powerful, and life-giving. Lord, let Your Word reveal the areas in my life that need to change. Give me the strength and discipline to turn away from anything that separates me from You, and help me to cling to what is true, pure, and right.

I desire to walk in Your ways, but I know I can't do it without You. Use Your Word to guide me, shape me, and prepare me for the work You've called me to do. Cleanse me, renew me, and continue making me into the woman You've created me to be. In Jesus' name, amen.

Reflect and Worship

🎵 Song Suggestion:
The Call
— Isabel Davis

As you listen to this song, be reminded that God's call on your life is intentional and filled with purpose. Seek His voice and lean into His guidance through worship on your favorite platform.

Reflection Prompt:

What verse can I meditate on today that speaks to where I am right now? How have I seen God use His Word to correct, encourage, or equip me recently?

Day 5:   While I Wait

Scripture: Psalm 40:1–2 (NLT)

"I waited patiently for the Lord to help me, and he turned to me and heard my cry. He lifted me out of the pit of despair, out of the mud and the mire. He set my feet on solid ground and steadied me as I walked along."

Dear Sis,

Waiting is one of the hardest things we're asked to do—but it's also one of the most powerful expressions of faith. Psalm 40 reminds us that when we wait patiently on the Lord, He not only hears our cries—He responds. He lifts us, restores us, and places us on solid ground.

We live in a world of instant results—microwaves, air fryers, same-day deliveries. But God is not in a rush. His timing is intentional and perfect. And while it may feel like you're stuck in the mud or drowning in despair, Sis, know this: God sees you. He hears you. And He is working behind the scenes.

Waiting on God doesn't mean doing nothing—it means trusting, praying, and preparing your heart while He does what only He can do. Don't give up in the wait. His hands are steadying your feet. He's making sure you don't just stand again—but that you walk forward in strength and purpose.

Prayer:
Strength While I Wait

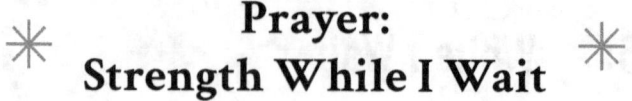

Father God,

Thank You for hearing my cries, even in the silence. Help me to wait patiently, trusting that You are working things out for my good.

I know that as long as I am living, there will be challenges—but Father, help me to turn to You with everything I'm facing, because I know that You have the answers. Your Word reminds me that when I cry out to You, You hear me—and I want to thank You for that. Thank You for the confidence to know that You always have my back and that You will always walk with me.

When I become frustrated or I don't understand, remind me to trust You—knowing that You have a plan, and it will all work together for my good. Strengthen my faith while I wait, and help me to stay steady in You. I trust You, Lord, and I lean on You. In Jesus' name, amen.

Reflect and Worship

♫ Song Suggestion:
Wait on You (featuring Dante Bowe & Chandler Moore)
— Elevation Worship & Maverick City Music

Sis, let this worship moment strengthen you as you wait on God. His timing is perfect, and His promises are sure. Search for the song on your preferred music platform and allow it to encourage your heart today.

Reflection Prompt:

What are you waiting on God for today? How can you strengthen your faith in the waiting season?

_____

_____

_____

_____

_____

_____

_____

_____

_____

_____

_____

_____

_____

_____

_____

_____

_____

_____

_____

_____

_____

Day 6: The Beauty of a God-Fearing Woman

Scripture: Proverbs 31:30 (NLT)
"Charm is deceptive, and beauty does not last;
but a woman who fears the Lord will be greatly praised."

Dear Sis,

Hallelujah! There's something powerful and beautiful about being a woman of God. The world may be obsessed with outward beauty and charm, but the Word reminds us that those things fade. What truly matters—what leaves a lasting legacy—is a heart that reverences the Lord.

It's okay to care about how you look—take care of yourself, adorn yourself with dignity and grace—but don't get so wrapped up in the outside that you neglect what's within. Your attitude, your character, your lifestyle, and your walk with God are what truly define your beauty.

Before writing this devotional, I asked my husband a question:
"Honey, what is one benefit of having a woman of God as your wife?"

He looked at me and said,
"I love that you genuinely pray for me. I've heard you pray for me out loud, and I know you cover me even when I'm not around. You keep me covered." That blessed me deeply.

Then I asked my children:
"What are the benefits of having a mom who loves the Lord?"
They answered: *"Mom, you teach us to pray and teach us about God."*

Sis, that's legacy. That's purpose. That's the fruit of being a woman who fears the Lord. When you walk with God, it shows—not just in your words, but in your life. So today, Sis—choose God. Live for Him. Stay with Him. Reverence Him in everything you do. There's no greater beauty than being a woman who walks closely with the Lord. That kind of beauty will never fade. Hallelujah!

Prayer:
Let My Life Reflect You

Father God,

Thank You for creating me with purpose and beauty—not just outwardly, but inwardly. Forgive me for the times I've focused more on appearances than on my walk with You. Teach me to fear You, to honor You, and to reflect Your love in everything I do. Help me to be a woman who leaves a lasting legacy of faith, who prays with power, loves with compassion, and lives with integrity. I know that as long as I am living, there will be challenges, but Father, help me to turn to You.

Your Word reminds me that You hear my cry, and I thank You for that. Thank You for the confidence to know that You always have my back and that You will walk with me. When I don't understand, I will trust that You have a plan—and that it will all work out for my good. I don't just want to look like a woman of God—I want to be one. In Jesus' name, amen.

Reflect and Worship

♫ Song Suggestion:
I Give Myself Away
— William McDowell

Sis, this song is a heartfelt surrender. Let it remind you that your life is a living offering to God. Find it on your favorite music platform and worship from a place of full devotion.

Reflection Prompt:

Am I more focused on how I look or how I live? What legacy of faith am I leaving for those who watch my life?

Day 7:   A Heart Like His

Scripture: Philippians 2:5 (NLT)
"You must have the same attitude that Christ Jesus had."

Dear Sis,

Wheww! This verse may be short, but it's *heavy!* That word "must" doesn't leave room for suggestions or maybes—it means it *needs* to be done. God is calling us to have the *same* attitude as Jesus. That means when situations arise, when people push our buttons, when life starts lifing—we are called to respond like Christ.

Let that sink in.

It's not always easy. In fact, it can feel downright impossible at times. But here's the good news, Sis: if God commands it, then by His Spirit—it can be done. The key is surrender. Daily. Not just once. Not just on Sundays. But every single day, we must choose to die to our flesh and let His character shine through us.

Choosing Christ's attitude means choosing love when it's hard, humility when pride wants to rise, and peace when chaos surrounds you. It's challenging, yes—but it's possible through His strength in you.

So today, Sis, decide to surrender. Lay down the need to respond your way and ask the Holy Spirit to lead the way. A Christ-like attitude will not only change how you deal with others—it will transform your heart.

Prayer: Transform Me, Lord

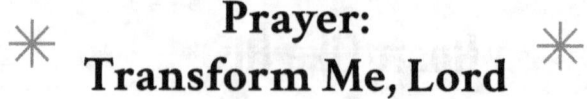

Father God,

I ask You to help me have the same attitude as Christ. Purify me. Cleanse me. Shape my heart, mind, and responses so they reflect Your character. Lord, especially when I come across people and situations that test me, I want to respond in love, grace, and humility—just like You would. I don't want to be less than who You've called me to be.

Father, I surrender my emotions, my opinions, and my reactions. Fill me with Your Spirit so that I can be the woman You've created me to be. Day by day, make me more like You. In Jesus' name, amen.

Reflect and Worship

♫ Song Suggestion:
More Like You
— Todd Galberth

Sis, let this song be your heart's cry today. Ask God to shape your thoughts, words, and actions so they mirror His love and character. Find it on your favorite music platform and worship through surrender.

Reflection Prompt:

Will you choose to surrender to God daily, so your attitude can reflect His?

Day 8: Choose Joy, Choose Prayer, Choose Thanks

Scripture: 1 Thessalonians 5:16–18 (NLT)

"Always be joyful. Never stop praying. Be thankful in all circumstances, for this is God's will for you who belong to Christ Jesus."

Dear Sis,

No matter what is going on in your life, no matter what you're facing, no matter how you feel in the moment—choose to look at things through a different lens. Choose joy. Choose to pray about everything. Choose to thank God, even when it's hard.

I'm not saying this because it sounds nice or because it's just some catchy motivational phrase. I'm saying it because God *commands* us to. He says, "Always be joyful, never stop praying, and be thankful in all circumstances." That's His will for us. And guess what? We *can* do it. We just have to make the choice.

It may not be easy, but it's possible. Do your best to rejoice, pray, and give thanks—and God will do the rest. He'll strengthen you, He'll carry you, and He'll help you see things from His perspective. When we choose joy, prayer, and gratitude, we align ourselves with God's will, and that's where the real peace and strength come from.

So, Sis, today—choose joy. Choose to pray. Choose to thank God, no matter the circumstance. When you do, you'll see how He'll move in your life.

Prayer:
Choosing Joy and Gratitude

Father God,

Thank You for reminding me of Your will for my life—to always be joyful, to never stop praying, and to be thankful in all circumstances. Lord, I choose joy today, even if I don't feel it right now. I choose to pray, knowing that You hear me and You care. I choose gratitude, even when life is hard, because I trust that You are working all things for my good.

Help me to see things through Your eyes and to walk in Your peace. Strengthen me to do my best, and I trust You to do the rest. In Jesus' name, amen.

Reflect and Worship

🎵 **Song Suggestion:**
When I Pray
— DOE

Sis, let this song remind you that your prayers are powerful and precious to God. No matter what you're going through, your voice matters in heaven. Look it up on your favorite music platform and let it stir your faith today.

Reflection Prompt:

How can you choose joy, prayer, and gratitude today, no matter what you are facing?

Day 9: Give It All to God

Scripture: 1 Peter 5:7 (NLT)
*"Give all your worries and cares to God,
for he cares about you."*

Dear Sis,

Give it all to God! There are times when people just can't fully understand what you're going through or how you feel. This is when you need to turn to God. He is the One who truly listens and understands the depths of your heart. No one knows you like He does.

When life feels overwhelming and your heart is heavy, run to Him in prayer. Tell God everything—pour your heart out, lay your worries and cares before Him, and trust that He will handle it in His perfect way. God is a good God. He is a God who cares deeply about you. He is the One who listens, who will never turn His back on you, and who understands you more than anyone else—more than you even understand yourself.

So, Sis, make it a habit to go to God first, with everything. No matter how big or small, He is there, ready and willing to listen and to carry your burdens. You don't have to carry them alone.

Prayer:
I Give It All to You

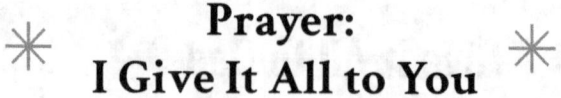

Father God,

I thank You for being a God who truly cares. Today, I give every worry, every fear, and every burden to You. You know my heart, You understand what I'm going through, and You care more than anyone else ever could.

Help me to remember that I don't have to carry these heavy things alone. You are always with me, listening to me, loving me, and working things out for my good. I trust You with every part of my heart, with my life, and with everything that weighs me down.

I surrender it all to You. Thank You for the peace that comes from knowing You've got it all under control. In Jesus' name, amen.

Reflect and Worship

♫ Song Suggestion:
Give Me You
— Shana Wilson

Sis, let this song become your heartfelt prayer today. Sometimes, all we really need is more of Him. Search for this worship moment on your favorite music platform and let it draw you closer to God's presence.

Reflection Prompt:

What are some worries or cares that you need to give to God today? How can you make it a habit to run to Him in prayer when you feel overwhelmed?

Day 10:   Stand Still and Watch God Work

Scripture: 2 Chronicles 20:17 (NLT)

"But you will not even need to fight. Take your positions; then stand still and watch the Lord's victory. He is with you, O people of Judah and Jerusalem. Do not be afraid or discouraged. Go out against them tomorrow, for the Lord is with you!"

Dear Sis,

There comes a time, after you've prayed and surrendered it all to the Lord, when your only assignment is to stand still. That's right—no fighting, no fixing, no explaining—just trust. God says, *"Take your position, stand still, and watch."*

Sis, sometimes the most powerful position you can take is silence and stillness. Hush your mouth. Don't say a word unless God tells you to. Don't move unless He leads you. Let God handle the situation however He sees fit.

You may feel the pressure to react, respond, or revisit the issue—but resist that temptation. Let the Holy Spirit guide you. Take your hands off it and let God put His hands on it. He's already promised to fight the battle for you, and when God fights—victory is guaranteed.

So stand tall in your faith. Be still in your spirit. And watch your faithful God move on your behalf.

Prayer: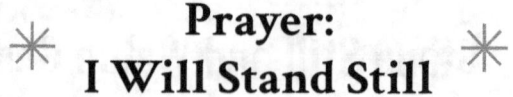
I Will Stand Still

Father God,

Thank You for the peace that gives me permission to sit this one out and trust You completely. I don't need all the details—I just need to know You're in control, and that's enough for me.

Lord, I resist the urge to act out of fear, frustration, or discouragement. Your Word tells me not to be afraid or discouraged, so I choose to stand still and trust You. Help me stay in position, to hold my peace, and to watch You bring the victory. I surrender this battle to You completely. In Jesus' name, amen.

Reflect and Worship

♫ Song Suggestion:
Work It Out
— Dr. Charles G. Hayes & The Warriors

Sis, this song is a reminder that God is already working behind the scenes. Even when you don't see it, He's moving. Search for it on your favorite music platform and let it stir your faith as you choose to stand still and trust Him.

Reflection Prompt:

Are you willing to take your hands off the situation and let God handle it? What does "standing still" look like for you today?

_____

_____

_____

_____

_____

_____

_____

_____

_____

_____

_____

_____

_____

_____

_____

_____

_____

_____

_____

_____

Day 11:   Make Room for Transformation

Scripture:

"Don't copy the behavior and customs of this world, but let God transform you into a new person by changing the way you think. Then you will learn to know God's will for you, which is good and pleasing and perfect."
— Romans 12:2 (NLT)

Dear Sis,

There are moments in life when we unknowingly pick up habits, mindsets, and patterns that don't reflect who God created us to be. Little by little, the world shapes our thinking, and before we know it, we're operating from a place that's not aligned with God's truth.

But here's the good news—God desires to *transform* us. Not just slightly improve us, but transform us into something entirely new. That transformation starts in the mind. When we invite Him in, He begins renewing our thoughts, shifting our perspective, and revealing His perfect will for our lives.

Sis, are you willing to make room for that kind of change? Are you ready to release old patterns and open yourself up to God's divine makeover? It's not always easy, but it is always worth it. Let's stop settling for what has been and start reaching for what God desires.

Come on—let's do this together. Let's make room for transformation.

Prayer:
A Prayer to Be Renewed

Father God, in the name of Jesus, I call on You to renew me. Renew me in the places I don't even know need renewing, and in the places, I do. I don't want to be like what I see around me—I want to be different. Help me to embrace a different and unique mindset, because I know that being Your child means being set apart.

Transform my thinking fully so I can know Your perfect will for my life and walk it out in confidence and obedience. When I see others around me adapting to worldly behaviors, customs, and attitudes, help me to respond with grace and love—praying for them in the same way I pray for myself. In Jesus' name, amen.

Reflect and Worship

♫ **Song Suggestion:**
Make Room
— Jonathan McReynolds

Sis, this song is a powerful reminder to clear out the clutter and give God full access to every part of your life. As you listen, ask Him to reveal anything taking up space that belongs to Him. Find it on your favorite music platform and let the message lead you into surrender.

Reflection Prompt:

What habits or mindsets have I unknowingly adopted that may be holding me back? Am I truly making space in my life for God to transform me?

Day 12: Wait on God

Scripture:
"Wait patiently for the Lord. Be brave and courageous.
Yes, wait patiently for the Lord."
— Psalm 27:14 (NLT)

Dear Sis,

Wait on God—yes, *patiently*. That's not always easy to do, especially when emotions rise and we feel pressure to act quickly or take matters into our own hands. But Sis, don't let your emotions lead you into decisions that God hasn't called you to make.

There is something powerful happening in the waiting. God is working behind the scenes—preparing, protecting, and positioning you for His best. Rushing ahead could mean missing out on what He's doing or delaying the blessings He has in store.

So be brave. Be courageous. And trust Him enough to be still. Keep reminding yourself: *Waiting is not wasted when it's in God's hands.*

Prayer:
A Prayer to Trust While I Wait

Father, help me to wait on You with patience and courage. When I feel anxious or overwhelmed, remind me that You are working things out for my good—even when I can't see it. I don't want to make decisions from a place of fear or emotion, but from a place of trust. Strengthen me to be still and know that You are God.

Even when I feel like moving, Holy Spirit, help me to be still and wait on God—because I know He has the best for me, and I want *His* best. I don't want to be moved by what I am facing, but instead I want to be moved, led, and guided by *Your* Spirit. Help me to see, hear, and know when You are speaking so that I can move accordingly. In Jesus' name, amen.

Reflect and Worship

♫ **Song Suggestion:**
Trust Him
— Tamela Mann

Sis, lean into this worship moment and be reminded that God can be trusted—even when things don't make sense. Let this song wash over your anxious thoughts and renew your confidence in His timing. Look it up on your favorite music platform and allow it to minister to your heart.

Reflection Prompt:

What area of my life am I tempted to rush instead of wait on God? How can I actively practice patience and trust while I wait?

Day 13: Praise Him on Purpose

Scripture:

"I will praise you, Lord, with all my heart; I will tell of all the marvelous things you have done. I will be filled with joy because of you. I will sing praises to your name, O Most High."

— Psalm 9:1–2 (NLT)

Dear Sis,

God is worthy of all our praise! He's been faithful, loving, merciful, and present—even when we didn't deserve it. Sometimes, life can feel overwhelming. Challenges arise, emotions weigh us down, and it's easy to forget just how good God has already been. But Sis, that's exactly when praise becomes powerful.

When we choose to praise God in the middle of our situation, it shifts our focus from what's wrong to *Who* is right—our Savior. Praise is our reminder that He's still in control, still moving, and still worthy.

So go ahead—speak of His goodness, shout your hallelujah, and say thank You, Jesus! Let your praise rise above your circumstances. He deserves it all!

Prayer:
A Praise-Filled Prayer

Father, I give You praise with my whole heart! You have done marvelous things in my life, and I refuse to stay silent. Even when my situation feels heavy, I choose to lift up Your name because You are good, and Your mercy endures forever.

Lord, thank You for every blessing, every door You've opened, and even the ones You've closed. Thank You for protecting me, guiding me, and loving me beyond measure. Help me to be a woman of praise—not just when things are going well, but at *all* times.

Even when tears are falling, I will lift my hands and say Hallelujah! Even when I don't understand, I will trust You and thank You. Fill my heart with joy and keep a song of praise on my lips. In Jesus' name, amen.

Reflect and Worship

♪ Song Suggestion:
Praise is What I Do
— William Murphy

Sis, even on the hard days, praise has the power to shift the atmosphere of your heart. This song is a beautiful reminder that praise is more than a feeling—it's a choice. Search for it on your favorite music platform and let it inspire you to worship through it all.

Reflection Prompt:

How can I intentionally choose praise even when I don't feel like it? What would my day look like if I started it with praise every morning?

Day 14:   Trust His Timing

Scripture:
"And we know that God causes everything to work together for the good of those who love God and are called according to his purpose for them."
— Romans 8:28 (NLT)

Dear Sis,

If God permitted it, then He will cause it all to work together for your good. It doesn't matter how difficult or confusing the situation may seem, God has a purpose for it, and His plan is good. Sometimes we may not understand why things happen, and that's okay. What matters is trusting Him.

We must trust His love for us, trust His perfect timing, and trust the process He's taking us through. His ways are higher than ours, and though we may not always see it, He is working everything out in our favor.

Stay connected to God. Stay in His Word. Keep praying. Trust that even in the hard moments, He's still at work—and He's working it all out for your good.

Prayer:
A Prayer to Trust His Plan

Father, I trust You today with everything in my life. Even when I don't understand, I trust that You are working everything out for my good. I trust Your love, Your timing, and Your process. Help me to remain steadfast in Your Word, to keep praying, and to trust that You have a purpose in every moment.

Father, forgive me for the times I didn't trust You and instead moved according to my own desires. Forgive me for acting out of fear or impatience, rather than waiting on Your guidance. I thank You for Your grace and mercy that lead and guide me daily. Thank You for not giving up on me and for showing me the way toward becoming a better version of myself. I am grateful for Your endless patience and unchanging love. In Jesus' name, amen.

Reflect and Worship

♫ Song Suggestion:
Surround Me O Lord
— Eddie James

Sis, when life feels uncertain, let this song be your prayer. Ask the Lord to surround you with His presence and peace. Look it up on your favorite music app, and let His nearness remind you that He's working everything out in His perfect timing.

Reflection Prompt:

What situations in my life do I need to surrender to God's timing and trust He is working them out for my good?

Day 15:   Trust and Delight

Scripture:
"Trust in the Lord and do good. Then you will live safely in the land and prosper. Take delight in the Lord, and He will give you your heart's desires. Commit everything you do to the Lord. Trust Him, and He will help you."
— Psalms 37:3-5 (NLT)

Dear Sis,

After reading these scriptures, go ahead and read them again. Let the words settle in. Take a moment to reflect on what they're saying to you. There are clear directions and promises within these verses. When you trust in the Lord and do good, you are promised peace, safety, and prosperity. When you delight in Him, He will give you the desires of your heart.

Did you catch it? Take a minute to see what God is speaking to you through this passage. Trust Him. Commit everything to Him. Delight in Him, and He will help you.

Sis, there's something powerful in simply trusting and delighting in God. It's a promise—He is faithful to help you and guide you in everything you do.

Prayer:
 # A Prayer of Trust and Delight

Lord, today I choose to trust You with everything I am and everything I have. I commit my ways to You. Help me to take delight in You and find joy in Your presence. I know that as I trust You and follow Your guidance, You will help me and give me the desires of my heart. Strengthen my faith, Lord, as I place my trust in You.

Father, I will commit myself fully to You and trust that You will help me along every step of my journey. Help me to hold on tightly to what Your Word says, and may Your promises be my anchor. Even in moments of doubt, remind me that You are faithful, that You are good, and that Your plans for me are always for my good.

I surrender my will to You and pray that You guide me, protect me, and equip me to walk in the path You've set before me. Let my trust in You be unshakable, and may my delight in Your presence fill my heart with peace and joy. In Jesus' name, amen.

Reflect and Worship

♫ Song Suggestion:
The One You Love (featuring Chandler Moore)
— Elevation Worship

Sis, you are deeply loved by God—never forget that. Let this song speak to your heart today. As you listen, remind yourself that the One who loves you can be trusted with every detail of your life. Look it up on your favorite music app and let it minister to you right where you are.

Reflection Prompt:

How can I actively trust God in all areas of my life?

Day 16:   My Only Hope Is in You

Scripture: Psalm 39:4–6 (NLT)

"Lord, remind me how brief my time on earth will be. Remind me that my days are numbered—how fleeting my life is. You have made my life no longer than the width of my hand. My entire lifetime is just a moment to you; at best, each of us is but a breath. We are merely moving shadows, and all our busy rushing ends in nothing. We heap up wealth, not knowing who will spend it. And so, Lord, where do I put my hope? My only hope is in you."

Dear Sis,

Life is short—fleeting, like a breath or a shadow that quickly disappears. These verses remind us just how temporary our time on earth really is. We get caught up in so much: the busyness, the rushing, the chasing after things that ultimately don't last. But at the end of it all, what really matters?

God gives each of us a choice. We get to choose how we live, who we serve, and where we place our hope. The world will offer temporary satisfaction, empty promises, and fleeting rewards. But God offers eternal life, peace, and purpose.

So Sis, today is a good day to pause and ask yourself: Where am I putting my hope? Is it in money, status, people, success—or is it in the One who created you for something far greater? Let your answer echo like David's: *"My only hope is in You, Lord."*

Prayer:
Remind Me What Matters

Father God,

In the name of Jesus, thank You for reminding me that my time on this earth is short and precious. Help me not to waste my life chasing after things that don't last. Lord, teach me to number my days and live each one with intention, purpose, and a heart that seeks after You.

I don't want to put my hope in people, possessions, or the pressures of this world. My only hope is in You. You are the One who gives meaning to my life. Keep me grounded in truth and focused on what truly matters. In Jesus' name, amen.

Reflect and Worship

🎵 Song Suggestion:
Lord You're Worthy
— New Direction

Sis, take a moment to remember the goodness of God. He is worthy of your trust, your praise, and your whole heart. As you worship, let this song shift your focus from the temporary to the eternal. Look it up on your favorite music platform and let your soul be anchored in hope.

Reflection Prompt:

If life is truly a breath, what can you start doing today to place your hope fully in the Lord?

Day 17:   I Will Never Run Out of Praise

Scripture: Psalm 40:5 (NLT)

"O Lord my God, you have performed many wonders for us. Your plans for us are too numerous to list. You have no equal. If I tried to recite all your wonderful deeds, I would never come to the end of them."

Dear Sis,

Hallelujah! God is so good—and He has done great and mighty things in our lives. Just pause and reflect: you've made it through things that should've taken you out. He's healed, provided, protected, and opened doors no one else could. And He's not done yet!

I love looking back at His faithfulness because it stirs my faith for what's ahead. It reminds me that if He did it before, He can and will do it again. We serve a limitless, matchless, wonder-working God—and there is no one like Him!

Sis, you may not see all the plans God has for you yet, but trust—they are too numerous to count. Keep praising Him, keep remembering, and keep watching for His hand in your life.

Prayer:
You've Done So Much for Me

Father God,

In the name of Jesus, I thank You for every wonderful work You've done in my life. You are mighty, faithful, and full of mercy. If I had 10,000 tongues, I still couldn't praise You enough for all You've brought me through.

Remind me to look back often—not with sorrow, but with gratitude. Let my heart stay filled with praise as I remember Your goodness. You've done so much for me, and I know You're not finished. I give You all the glory, honor, and praise. In Jesus' name, amen.

Reflect and Worship

♪ Song Suggestion:
Without You
— Tasha Cobbs Leonard

Sis, this song is a powerful reminder that we are nothing without the presence of God. As you listen, let gratitude rise up in your heart for all He's brought you through. Search for it on your favorite music platform and let it lead you into a moment of pure praise.

Reflection Prompt:

Take a moment to write down 3 things God has done for you that you never want to forget. Let it stir your praise!

Day 18:   Let Go of the Worry

Scripture: Matthew 6:27 (NLT)

"Can all your worries add a single moment to your life?"

Dear Sis,

Worrying doesn't help. It doesn't fix anything, heal anything, or change anything. All it does is weigh you down and drain your peace. That's why Jesus reminds us—*worry can't add a single moment to our lives.*

So, what should we do instead? Pray. Cast every care onto the Lord. He's not asking you to carry the weight of your world—He's asking you to trust Him with it.

Sis, it's time to shift. Don't get consumed by anxious thoughts. Get consumed by the presence of God. Go deeper in prayer. Find strength in His Word. When worry tries to creep in, fight back with worship, with Scripture, and with the truth that your Father is in control.

Prayer:
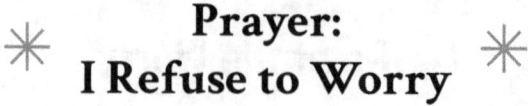
I Refuse to Worry

Father God,

In the name of Jesus, I give every worry to You. I know that worrying won't change anything, but prayer will. So I surrender every anxious thought, every fear, and every burden into Your hands.

Help me to remember that You care deeply for me and that You are always working things out for my good. Instead of being consumed by worry, let me be consumed by Your peace and presence. I trust You, Lord—and I refuse to worry. In Jesus' name, amen.

Reflect and Worship

♫ Song Suggestion:
Something Has To Break (featuring Tasha Cobbs Leonard)
— Kierra Sheard

Sis, sometimes the breakthrough begins with surrender. Let this song remind you that when God steps in, everything changes. Search for it on your preferred music app and allow it to speak to the situation you're releasing to Him.

Reflection Prompt:

What's something you've been worrying about that you can give to God today? Write it down, and then release it in prayer.

Day 19: It Will Work Out

Scripture: Romans 8:28 (NLT)

"And we know that God causes everything to work together for the good of those who love God and are called according to his purpose for them."

Dear Sis,

It will work out for your good. You may not see it now, and you may not understand why you're going through this, but God has a plan. Even in the pain. Even in the confusion. Even in the delay.

Sometimes life feels like a puzzle with missing pieces, but when you love God and are walking in His purpose, nothing is wasted. Not the tears. Not the waiting. Not the closed doors. It's all working together for something beautiful.

One day, you'll look back and say, "Wow, I didn't know how or when, but God really did it!" And He will. He's faithful. Keep trusting. Keep believing. It will happen.

Prayer:
You're Working Behind the Scenes

Father God,

In the name of Jesus, thank You for the promise that everything will work together for my good. Even when I don't see it or feel it, I believe You are working behind the scenes.

Strengthen my faith when doubt creeps in. Remind me that You are the God who keeps His promises. I trust You, Lord, with this season of my life. I trust You with my future. Help me to keep walking in Your purpose and leaning into Your love. You've never failed me, and I know You won't start now. In Jesus' name, amen.

Reflect and Worship

♬ Song Suggestion:
At Just The Right Time
— ONE HOUSE, Chandler Moore & Roosevelt Stewart

Sis, God's timing is never off. This song is a reminder that He shows up exactly when we need Him most. Look it up on your favorite music platform and let it encourage your heart today.

Reflection Prompt:

What is one situation in your life right now that you need to trust God is working out for your good?

Day 20: Worth the Wait

Scripture: Psalm 27:14 (NLT)
"Wait patiently for the Lord. Be brave and courageous.
Yes, wait patiently for the Lord."

Dear Sis,

You're waiting. You're wondering. "God, when?" It feels like time is standing still and your prayers are hanging in the air. The waiting season can feel like the hardest season. But sis, don't move ahead of God.

Don't give up. Don't compromise. Don't settle just to say it's done. God's best is worth the wait. The enemy wants you to believe that it'll never happen. But God says, *"Be brave. Be courageous. Wait on Me."* You will not regret trusting Him.

It may take longer than you hoped, but it will be better than you imagined. Let your waiting be worship. Let your patience be praise. Hold on a little longer—your blessing is closer than you think.

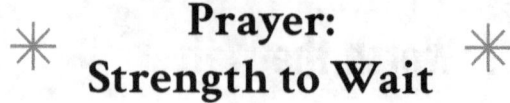

Prayer:
Strength to Wait

Father God,

In the name of Jesus, I thank You for being a faithful and trustworthy God. Waiting isn't always easy, but I know that Your timing is perfect.

Help me not to grow weary or give up while I wait. Give me courage to trust You, strength to endure, and faith to believe that what You have for me is worth it. I choose to wait on You, knowing that You are working behind the scenes and preparing something good. Thank You for loving me enough to make me wait. In Jesus' name, amen.

Reflect and Worship

🎵 **Song Suggestion:**
Evidence (featuring Naomi Raine)
— ReFRESH Worship

Sis, there is evidence of God's faithfulness all around you—even in the waiting. As you listen to this song, let your heart be reminded that He's working behind the scenes. Find it on your favorite music platform and let it encourage your trust.

Reflection Prompt:

What are you currently waiting on God for? Write it down, and ask Him to strengthen your heart as you wait.

Day 21: Divine Shelter

Scripture: Psalms 18:2 NLT

"The Lord is my rock, my fortress, and my savior; my God is my rock, in whom I find protection. He is my shield, the power that saves me, and my place of safety."

Dear Sis,

Hallelujah! Look at who God is to us—our rock, our fortress, our Savior, our protector, our shield, the One whose power saves us, and our place of safety. What a mighty and loving God we serve! When life feels shaky, uncertain, or overwhelming, remember this: you are never unprotected. You have a divine fortress wrapped around you. God is your safe place. He is everything you need and more. Let this truth strengthen you today. Rest in His love. Rest in His power. Rest in His protection. Yes, Sis—God is good!

Even when you feel alone, He surrounds you. Even when fear tries to grip your heart, His presence will steady you. His promises are not just comforting—they are covering. Stand tall today, knowing that your God has you completely covered, inside and out.

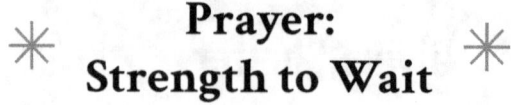

Prayer:
Strength to Wait

Father God,

In the name of Jesus, thank You for being my rock and my fortress. You are the One I run to when I need shelter. Thank You for protecting me from the things I see and the things I don't. When I feel overwhelmed, remind me that You are my shield and my place of safety. I trust You to be everything I need, right when I need it. Thank You for never leaving me uncovered. I rest in You today, Lord. In Jesus' name, amen.

Reflect and Worship

♫ Song Suggestion:
Crashing
— Phil Thompson

Sis, when life feels chaotic or uncertain, let this song be a reminder that God is your safe place. Even when everything feels like it's crashing around you, He is steady, faithful, and close. Search for this song on your favorite music platform, and let it wash over your heart with peace.

Reflection Prompt:

What does it mean to you personally to have God as your place of safety?

Day 22: Choose Freedom Through Forgiveness

Proverbs 17:9 NLT

"Love prospers when a fault is forgiven,
but dwelling on it separates close friends."

Dear Sis,

Just let it go. Forgive. People will be people—no one is perfect. Stop replaying the offense in your mind. Stop carrying what God is calling you to release. Forgive. Don't you want God to forgive you? Then do the same. It's okay to re-position someone in your life and love them from a distance—but forgive. No one is worth you missing out on what God has for you.

Forgiveness doesn't mean what they did was okay—it simply means you're choosing freedom. You're choosing to release the weight of what happened and hand it over to God. Free yourself, Sis. Let God heal you, restore you, and handle the rest. Your Heavenly Father sees it all. He understands the hurt, and He loves you deeply.

Prayer: Strength to Wait

Father God,

In the name of Jesus, help me to forgive those who have hurt me. It still hurts, and I don't always know how to move forward—but I know You will help me. You are my Healer. Father, I recognize that I am not perfect. I've sinned and asked You for forgiveness, and You extended Your mercy to me. Help me to offer that same grace to others.

I don't want bitterness or pain to take over the beauty You've placed in me. Heal my heart, Lord. Remove the weight and renew my spirit. Thank You for understanding, and for always loving.

Reflect and Worship

🎵 **Song Suggestion:**
Healer
— William Murphy

Sis, healing often begins with forgiveness. As you listen to this powerful song, allow God to mend the places in your heart that have been wounded. Whether it's forgiving someone else or even yourself, trust that God is your healer. Look it up on your favorite music platform and let Him begin (or continue) the work in you.

Reflection Prompt:

Is there someone you need to forgive today so you can be free?

Day 23: Blessings Are Closer Than You Think

Scripture:
Amos 9:11–15 MSG

"But also on that Judgment Day I will restore David's house that has fallen to pieces. I'll repair the holes in the roof, replace the broken windows, fix it up like new... Things are going to happen so fast your head will swim, one thing fast on the heels of the other. You won't be able to keep up. Everything will be happening at once—and everywhere you look, blessings!... They'll never again be uprooted from the land I've given them."
God, your God, says so.

Dear Sis,

I prophesy: Any Day Now! Hallelujah!

Receive it. Hold on to it. Declare it over your life—Any Day Now!

Did you catch that? Do you feel it in your spirit? Any Day Now—the breakthrough, the restoration, the answer to your long-awaited prayer. The time is coming, and it's closer than you think. What's been broken will be rebuilt. What's been lost will be returned. What's been delayed will be delivered—right on time!

Blessings are lining up with your name on them. God's hand is moving behind the scenes, arranging every detail, restoring what was once shattered, and fulfilling what He promised. Sis, get ready—Any Day Now!

Prayer:
Strength to Wait

Father God,

In the mighty name of Jesus, I receive this Word. I believe that Any Day Now You will move mightily in my life. I trust that restoration is coming. The things I've cried about, prayed about, fasted for—You are about to release them into my hands.

Thank You for the promise of overflow. I won't miss it. I won't doubt it. I will stand in faith and expectation. Let my heart stay aligned with You as You begin to move in miraculous ways. I'm ready, Lord. Any Day Now! In Jesus' name, amen.

Reflect and Worship

♫ Song Suggestion:
All of a Sudden (featuring Tiffany Hudson & Chris Brown)
— Elevation Worship

Sis, sometimes God shows up all of a sudden—just when you least expect it, but right when you need it. Let this song stir your hope and expectation. Look it up on your favorite music platform and believe that your breakthrough could be just around the corner.

Reflection Prompt:

What are you believing God to do any day now? Write it down. Declare it in faith. Expect it.

Day 24:   It's a Wonderful Life

Scripture:
Psalms 73:28 AMP

"But as for me, it is good for me to draw near to God;
I have made the Lord God my refuge and placed my trust in Him,
That I may tell of all Your works."

Dear Sis,

Sis, let me tell you—there's nothing like drawing near to the Lord! It is truly a wonderful life. God is my refuge, the One I run to when life gets hectic, and the One I talk to when things are good. He is my everything! Hallelujah!

I've decided, day by day, to trust in Him. He has never failed me. Hallelujah! It's a wonderful life indeed, filled with peace and joy. Can I just tell you? I've been feeling and loving my Jesus more deeply than ever. His presence is transforming me from the inside out. Sis, I encourage you to do the same—draw near to Him. Keep the conversation going with Him. He's faithful, and He is good. Your trust in Him will never be misplaced.

Prayer:
I Choose to Draw Near

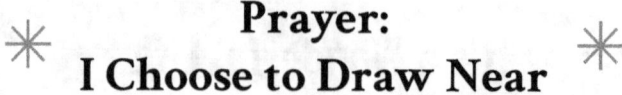

Father God,

As I look back on my life, I see how faithful You've been. Even in moments when I didn't recognize it, You were there, working on my behalf. Thank You for Your love, Your guidance, and Your protection. I want to be consistent in drawing near to You. I long for that close, intimate communion with You.

Today, I make the choice to trust You completely, even in moments of uncertainty. You are my refuge, and I place my trust in You fully. I commit to telling those around me of Your wonderful works, because You are so amazing!

I love You, Lord. Thank You for being my safe place.
In Jesus' name, amen.

Reflect and Worship

🎵 **Song Suggestion:**
Take It To Jesus
— Johnny Ruffin Jr

Sis, when life feels heavy and uncertain, remember you can always take it to Jesus. He is your safe place, your peace, and your refuge. Look this one up on your favorite music app and let it remind you that you don't have to carry it alone.

Reflection Prompt:

Where do you need to draw near to God today? How can you make Him your refuge in your current circumstances?

Day 25: Faithful Anyway

Scripture:
Psalms 78:21–25 AMP

"Therefore, when the Lord heard, He was full of wrath; A fire was kindled against Jacob, and His anger mounted up against Israel, Because they did not believe in God [they did not rely on Him, they did not adhere to Him], And they did not trust in His salvation (His power to save). Yet He commanded the clouds from above And opened the doors of heaven; And He rained down manna upon them to eat And gave them the grain of heaven. Man ate the bread of angels; God sent them provision in abundance."

Dear Sis,

God is merciful. These verses show us that even when the people didn't trust or believe in Him, God *still* provided for them. Wow. That truth humbles me. It reminds me that we serve a God full of grace and compassion.

This passage stirs something in me—it makes me want to do better. It urges me to check my heart and reflect on the areas where I haven't fully trusted God. No, I'm not perfect, and neither are you, but we can make the intentional choice to lean on Him more deeply. God is our Provider, our Sustainer, and He deserves our faith and reliance.

Prayer:
Strength to Wait

Father God,

Thank You for Your mercy and for continuing to provide even when we fall short. Forgive me for the times I've leaned on my own understanding instead of trusting You fully. Lord, I don't want to walk in unbelief—I want to rely on You in all things.

Teach me to trust You more with every area of my life. Help me to remember that You are faithful, and Your provision never fails. I choose to depend on You. Thank You for being so good to me, even when I didn't deserve it.

In Jesus' name, amen.

Reflect and Worship

♫ Song Suggestion:
You Are Here
— William McDowell

Sis, no matter what you're facing, know this—God is here. Right now. Right where you are. Let this song wash over you as a reminder of His presence. Search for it on your favorite music platform and let it lead you into deeper trust.

Reflection Prompt:

Are there any areas in your life where you've been struggling to fully trust God? What step can you take today to rely more on His provision?

Day 26:   Met in the Moment

Scripture:
Isaiah 41:13 AMP
""For I the Lord your God keep hold of your right hand; [I am the Lord],
Who says to you, 'Do not fear, I will help you.'"

Dear Sis,

I was lying in bed praying and asking God to help me parent my boys. Then I picked up my phone to read the verse of the day—and it was this one. Isaiah 41:13. I love it! God is so real. He met me right where I was and gave me exactly what I needed in that moment.

I have good kids, and I thank God for them, but I still need His help raising them. I understand that my role as a parent is not something I do alone—I need to partner with God to guide them in the direction of His will for their lives. This verse reminded me to breathe, to let go of fear, and to trust that I have God's help. Hallelujah. Thank You, Jesus!

Sis, whatever you're bringing to God in prayer—whether it's your children, your health, your future, or your pain—please know that He is present. Just like He met me while I was lying in bed, He will meet you right where you are. God wants to walk closely with you. He wants to be invited into every part of your life. All we have to do is say, "Yes, Lord."

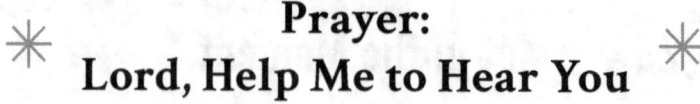

Prayer:
Lord, Help Me to Hear You

Father God, thank You for being near in moments of weakness, uncertainty, and fear. Thank You for speaking so clearly and personally when I call on You. I am grateful that I don't have to do life alone—I have You.

Help me to always recognize Your voice, even in the noise. Help me not to let my circumstances drown out Your truth. I want to partner with You in every area of my life. Teach me to trust You more, and to rest in Your promise that You will help me.

In Jesus' name, amen.

Reflect and Worship

♫ Song Suggestion:
Never Run Dry
— Casey J

Sis, when you feel depleted or uncertain, remember—God's well of grace, strength, and wisdom will never run dry. Look up this song on your favorite music app and let it refill your soul with hope and confidence in His supply.

Reflection Prompt:

What area of your life do you need to intentionally invite God into today? How can you create space to listen for His help and direction?

Day 27:   The Power of Your Yes

Scripture:
Psalms 84:11-12 AMP

"For the Lord God is a sun and shield; The Lord bestows grace and favor and honor; No good thing will He withhold from those who walk uprightly. O Lord of hosts, How blessed and greatly favored is the man who trusts in You [believing in You, relying on You, and committing himself to You with confident hope and expectation]."

Dear Sis,

Amen and hallelujah! There is such power in not just knowing God as Savior—but allowing Him to be Lord over every area of your life. There is a difference! Yes, salvation is the beautiful gift of grace, but lordship is a daily decision. And with that decision comes benefits and blessings beyond what we can imagine.

God desires to be your sun and your shield—your light in dark places and your protection when things come against you. When you choose to trust Him, walk uprightly, and commit to His ways, He promises that no good thing will be withheld from you. That's favor. That's grace. That's His divine covering over your life.

Sis, we are blessed and highly favored simply because we've made the choice to trust in the Lord. He's waiting to pour out even more, but it begins with your yes.

Prayer:
Lord, I Surrender to Your Lordship

Father, help me take this walk with You seriously. I know You have so much You want to release into my life, but You're waiting for me to step into full surrender. I don't want to hold anything back. I want to receive the blessings You have prepared for me.

Today, I surrender my whole heart, my whole life, and every area of concern into Your hands. You are not only my Savior—but You are my Lord. I trust You, and I will walk in confident expectation of what You have in store.

In Jesus' name, amen.

Reflect and Worship

♫ Song Suggestion:
Gracefully Broken
— Tasha Cobbs Leonard

Sis, full surrender can be hard, but it's where healing and transformation begin. Let this song guide your heart to a posture of openness before God. Search for it on your go-to music platform and allow the lyrics to lead you into deeper trust.

Reflection Prompt:

Will that be you? Are you ready to experience the abundant life God promises to those who fully surrender and trust Him as Lord?

Day 28:   Stand Still, Sis

Scripture:
Psalms 46:10 AMP

"Be still and know (recognize, understand) that I am God.
I will be exalted among the nations! I will be exalted in the earth."

Dear Sis,

There will be moments and seasons when you've done all you can. You've prayed, fasted, cried, believed—and now the Lord says, *Be still.*

Stand still, sis. Let God move how He wants to move. This is the part where your trust is tested—not in your doing, but in your waiting.

During this time, I encourage you to stay anchored in His Word, keep showing up in His presence, and continue believing what God has spoken over your life. Your *suddenly* is closer than you think! Hallelujah! Praise God in advance!

Don't give up. Don't compromise. Don't try to fix it in your own strength. God's timing is perfect. He knows exactly what He's doing and when He's going to do it. Be still—and know.

Prayer:
Lord, I Surrender to Your Lordship

Father, help me to be still when everything in me wants to take control. Help me to resist the urge to interfere or make something happen on my own. I don't want to mess up what You're putting together.

I believe in Your promises and I trust in Your perfect timing. I command my emotions and my flesh to submit to Your Spirit. I will wait on You, Lord. Lead me, guide me, and strengthen me as I wait.

In Jesus' name, amen.

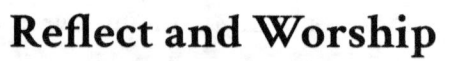

Reflect and Worship

♫ Song Suggestion:
Spirit Break Out (featuring Trinity Anderson)
— William McDowell

Sis, sometimes breakthrough doesn't come in noise, but in stillness. Let this worship moment invite the Spirit of God to move in your heart while you stay rooted in trust. Look it up on your favorite music platform and allow the lyrics to gently usher you into surrender.

Reflection Prompt:

Where in your life is God asking you to be still? Are you willing to surrender control and trust His timing, even when it's hard?

Day 29: Ask for Help

Scripture:
Psalms 37:5 NLT
"Commit everything you do to the Lord. Trust him, and he will help you."

Dear Sis,

This morning during my quiet time, I was meditating on this verse and asking God for help with a few things. So clearly, I heard Him whisper, *"I love when you ask for My help. It lets Me see that you don't want to do it alone."* Whew! I immediately began to cry. There is something so beautiful about inviting God into everything. I want His help—so I go to Him with everything.

Sis, let me encourage you to do the same. Ask God for help. Don't hesitate. He wants to be involved in every detail of your life. And guess what? He loves when you ask! You don't have to do it on your own. The scripture gives us the perfect prescription: Commit. Trust. He will help. Now let's take it—daily.

Prayer:
✳ # I Will Ask for Help ✳

Father, thank You for showing me a daily prescription I can live by—commit, trust, and You will help. Let that truth be written on my heart. Remind me to humble myself before You and invite You in, every single day. I don't want to move ahead of You. I want to walk with You. Thank You for loving me enough to help me when I ask. In Jesus' name, amen.

Reflect and Worship

🎵 **Song Suggestion:**
Surround (Fight My Battles) (featuring James Fortune)
— Lasha' Knox

Sis, no matter what you're facing, remember: the battle belongs to the Lord. Let this powerful worship moment remind you that you're not alone. Search for it on your go-to music platform, and allow God to surround you with His strength and peace.

Reflection Prompt:

What area of your life do you need to fully commit to the Lord today? Will you trust Him to help you with it?

Day 30:   Don't Peek—Just Trust

Scripture:
Proverbs 3:5-6 NLT –
"Trust in the Lord with all your heart; do not depend on your own understanding. Seek his will in all you do, and he will show you which path to take."

Dear Sis,

Let me be transparent! There are areas in my life where I struggle fully to trust God. I believe many of us may have an area like that. But let's put forth much effort to fully trust God in those areas—our weak areas. Let's do what the scriptures are speaking to us. Let's keep praying. Let's keep trusting. I want to leave you with a "life nugget" I received from a woman of God I met during a visit to pick up a pizza for my family. She said to me, "Walk behind God and don't disturb Him. Trust God!" That was so powerful! In life, we have to be willing to walk behind God and stop trying to peek around His shoulders and see what is ahead. We have to trust Him. Don't disturb what He is trying to do. Trust Him. ·

When we try to get ahead of God, we risk missing the beauty of His perfect plan. His timing is intentional, and His way is always better. Even in uncertainty, His path is sure. Let today be the day you release control and walk by faith—one surrendered step at a time.

Prayer:
Trusting God in Weak Areas

Father,

Help me to trust you in those weak areas of mine. I have leaned to my own understanding, and it didn't work for me. I want to seek your will in everything I do, but I need your help. I want to take that life nugget and apply it to every area of my life. I want to trust you more and stop trying to peek and understand what is ahead in my life and my loved ones. I am simply choosing to trust you and give up leaning to my own understanding in Jesus name, amen.

Reflect and Worship

🎵 **Song Suggestion:**
I Surrender x JGM (cover)
— Jordan G. Welch

Sis, true freedom begins with surrender. Let this heartfelt song lead you into a moment of release, where you give God full access to your heart. Look it up on your favorite music app, and let the message soften your spirit and build your trust.

Reflection Prompt:

Where do you struggle most in trusting God? What steps can you take to let go and trust Him more fully in those areas??

Day 31:   Fight for Your Family

Scripture:
Nehemiah 4:14 NLT
*Then as I looked over the situation, I called together the nobles and
the rest of the people and said to them, "Don't be afraid of the enemy!
Remember the Lord, who is great and glorious, and fight for
your brothers, your sons, your daughters, your wives, and your homes!"*

Dear Sis,

Don't be afraid. Stand firm and fight for your family and your home.
Stay vigilant and aware of what's happening within your household.
Never allow the enemy to gain a foothold in your family's life. Fight
for your loved ones—ask God for wisdom and strategies to protect and
strengthen your home. Walk in love, keep peace, and be steadfast in
guarding what God has blessed you with. Remember, God's power is far
greater than any opposition. Hallelujah!

Keep your heart focused and your faith strong. Speak life over your
home each day. Trust that God is working in ways you may not yet see,
but He is always faithful.

Prayer:
Fighting for Family

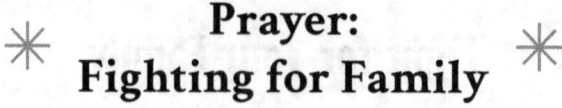

Father,

Thank You for being the perfect example of a love that never gives up. You fought for me and continue to fight on my behalf. I want to stand in that same strength for myself and my family. Thank You for the grace and power to love my family through the challenges. I speak victory over my household and declare peace over my home and everyone connected to me. In Jesus' name, amen.

Reflect and Worship

🎵 **Song Suggestion:**
Worth Fighting For
— Brian Courtney Wilson

Sis, your family, your peace, and your purpose are worth fighting for. Let this song be your anthem today. Search for it on your favorite music platform and let God remind you that He is with you in the battle.

Reflection Prompt:

What are some ways you can actively fight for your family and home? How can you seek God's strategies and maintain peace in your household?

A Final Word   But Not Goodbye!

Dear Sis,

You made it—and I am so proud of you.

You stuck with it even when things got hard. You pushed through even when you wanted to give up. That speaks volumes about your strength, your faith, and the God who's been walking with you every step of the way.

Sis, I want you to keep going.

Let this devotional be a reminder of how far you've come and the truth that God is not finished with you yet. Revisit it anytime you need to be refreshed. If and when you do, I promise—God will meet you right there.

This journey of faith, hope, and healing is lifelong. But you're never alone. I'm praying you keep trusting Him, keep showing up, and keep letting God's love carry you forward. The same God who met you on Day 1 will continue to guide you through every chapter of your life.

You are seen. You are loved. You are chosen.

And Sis, you've got this—because God's got you.

Scripture:
"I am sure of this, that He who started a good work in you will carry it on to completion until the day of Christ Jesus."
—Philippians 1:6 (CSB)

✳ **Prayer:** ✳

Father, thank You for being with my sister throughout this journey. Thank You for every breakthrough, every tear, every moment of peace, and every whisper of truth You've spoken to her heart. I pray that she continues to walk in confidence, knowing that You are not done with her. Strengthen her when she feels weak. Remind her of Your promises when doubts try to creep in. Lead her deeper into intimacy with You. Fill her life with joy, healing, and a greater understanding of who she is in You. May she never forget this sacred time we shared—one sister to another. Bless her, Father, and continue the beautiful work You've started in her. In Jesus' name, amen.

www.ingramcontent.com/pod-product-compliance
Lightning Source LLC
Chambersburg PA
CBHW070339130626
46556CB00007B/2932